MW01174670

Happy Anniversary!

To

Chrisy + Tino

From

Mary, Don + family

Date

Happy Anniversary!

hugs
eXPression
of the **Heart** ™

Happy Anniversary!

HOWARD BOOKS
A DIVISION OF SIMON & SCHUSTER
New York   London   Toronto   Sydney

Our purpose at Howard Books is to:
- •*Increase faith* in the hearts of growing Christians
- •*Inspire holiness* in the lives of believers
- •*Instill hope* in the hearts of struggling people everywhere

Because He's coming again!

Published by Howard Books, a division of Simon & Schuster
1230 Avenue of the Americas, New York, NY 10020
www.howardpublishing.com

HOWARD
BOOKS

Happy Anniversary! © 2006 by Howard Books

ISBN 10: 1-58229-671-5; ISBN 13: 978-1-58229-671-5
ISBN 10: 1-4165-3584-5; ISBN 13: 978-1-4165-3584-3

10   9   8   7   6   5   4   3   2   1

HOWARD colophon is a registered trademark of Simon & Schuster, Inc.

Manufactured in China

For information regarding special discounts for bulk purchases, please contact Simon & Schuster Special Sales at 1-800-456-6798 or business@simonandschuster.com.

Contributors: Angie Kiesling, Gary Myers, Debbie Webb, Philis Boultinghouse
Edited by Philis Boultinghouse
Cover design by Terry Dugan Design
Interior design by Stephanie D. Walker and Tennille Paden

Contents

Affection

Never Forget

Near to Me

Inspiration

Vision

Enjoyment

Realization

Sweetheart

Adoration

Romance

Yesteryear

CHAPTER 1

Affection

The intertwining of two hearts is a fearful yet beautiful thing. Who but God could have orchestrated such a divine melody, where each person plays to the tune he or she hears in the other?

On this anniversary of love, remember that this is a forever kind of love. Being a part of marriage makes each one a better person, a braver person, each completing the other.

I'm so glad God is still a matchmaker.

Happy anniversary!

ANNIVERSARY

AND THINK NOT YOU CAN
GUIDE THE COURSE OF LOVE.
FOR LOVE, IF IT FINDS YOU WORTHY,
SHALL GUIDE YOUR COURSE.

Khalil Gibran

● Sonnet 43 ●

How do I love thee? Let me count the ways.
I love thee to the depth and breadth and height
My soul can reach, when feeling out of sight
For the ends of Being and ideal Grace.

I love thee to the level of every day's
Most quiet need, by sun and candlelight.
I love thee freely, as men strive for right;
I love thee purely, as they turn from praise.

I love thee with the passion put to use

In my old griefs, and with my childhood's faith.

I love thee with a love I seemed to lose

With my lost saints—I love thee with the breath,

Smiles, tears, of all my life!—and, if God choose,

I shall but love thee better after death.

Elizabeth Barrett Browning

Let *love* and *faithfulness* never leave you; *bind* them around your NECK, *write* them on the tablet of your *heart*.

Proverbs 3:3

Affection

Never Forget

Near to Me

Inspiration

Vision

Enjoyment

Realization

Sweetheart

Adoration

Romance

Yesteryear

CHAPTER 2

Never Forget

Everyone talks of true love as if it were a magic potion granted to only a few fortunate souls on earth. The secret to lasting love can be discovered by searchers. In learning to forgive comes also learning to forget—but only the things that need forgetting.

Like a never-fading rose pressed between the pages of life's story, love grows older and wiser with each passing year. The small wonders, the impromptu words of love, the expressions that become etched on the mind—these are the things we should never forget, ever.

ANNIVERSARY

THE HEART'S MEMORY
ELIMINATES THE BAD AND
MAGNIFIES THE GOOD;
AND THANKS TO THIS ARTIFICE
WE MANAGE TO ENDURE
THE BURDENS OF THE PAST.

Gabriel García Márquez

True love is loving
in spite of imperfection.
True love is accepting
each other's flawed states and
choosing to build a strong and
committed relationship anyway.

Marilyn Meberg

◦ A Hidden Blessing ◦

Kim dropped into bed exhausted, as usual. What had started as a hobby had ended up as an all-consuming occupation.

She'd always had a heart for animals. "Kim has brought home more stray dogs and homeless cats than the humane society has rescued in their entire history," her mother loved to say when she was young. But Kim couldn't resist the helplessness of abandoned animals. Her keen, compassionate eyes were always scanning for furry little fugitives needing a sympathetic patron.

Now she was grown with a family of her own; her hands full of responsibility, her head full of figures, her heart full of family, and her hours full of activity. In the beginning, she had stumbled into a dog-and-cat-sitting business quite accidentally. Friends had imposed upon her generous spirit and her love for animals when they needed to go out of town, leaving her to manage all types and temperaments of four-footed creatures. Carl, her husband, had suggested that she advertise and at least get paid for the time and trouble it was costing her; in fact, he'd said, costing the whole family.

Over time her business had flourished into a full-fledged kennel, complete with pet hospitalization and burial services. The bookkeeping and grounds management alone kept her in over her head, not to mention the precarious situations that tend to come up when you mix dogs, cats, medicine, and people.

Kim knew she had asked a lot of her family. They were all active participants in the business, from the head of the household to the tiniest toddler. The hours spent caring for the animals took the time they could have spent playing games and taking walks. The days they might have spent visiting the zoo or shopping at the mall were dedicated to grooming Afghan hounds and treating kittens for ringworm. But Carl and the kids had always been right there with her, never complaining, never looking back. They were totally committed, so at least they were together as a family all the time. And it was Carl she could thank for that. He had jumped in with her as a partner, though he had a full-time career of his own, and the kids had taken their cue from their father.

Today had been the most difficult that Kim could

remember since the kennel had begun. There had been a scandal over the death of a wealthy woman's black Lab, which ended in a threat of litigation. The poor dog was old, despondent, and dying. But his owner was convinced that he only had a slight case of arthritis. When she discovered that the dog had died in Kim's kennel the second night of his stay, she went into a frenzied state of hysteria and ran all the way to her car screaming, "Murderers! You thieving murderers!"

The threat of a lawsuit scared Jim, the staff veterinarian, so badly that he turned in his resignation before the end of his shift. What a fiasco the day had been.

It was late when Kim closed the door on the last kennel cage. The puppies were finally quiet. The kids were in bed after prayers had been said without her. She hadn't even been with them for supper because there was so much to do in Jim's absence. Kim felt a slight indignation toward Carl over the fact that he had acted a little sullen about her absence from the family outing. He had suggested a quick run to the family-style restaurant off Highway 44 when it became apparent to him that Kim wouldn't have time to cook. Shaking her head as she trotted off to the shed to look for a replacement for a broken leash, she waved him off irritably. Couldn't he see she was swamped? How insensitive can a man get?

After a quick, hot bath to relax her aching back, Kim dropped into bed frazzled and weary beside Carl, who was snoring faintly in a deep sleep.

It was nearly midnight. Kim was rehearsing some bookkeeping tasks that hadn't been completed when she remembered today's date. With a jolt of sudden remorse, she realized that tomorrow was their anniversary and she had completely forgotten. In the midst of her turmoil, Kim's priorities had been ambushed, and she was taken prisoner by the urgent. Tears of frustration stung her eyes as an overwhelming urge to break and run swelled in her heart.

Of all people, Carl deserved to be remembered, even if he pouted from time to time. He had always been there for her. He had always come through. She turned to see his profile as he lay sleeping next to her in the bed they had shared these fifteen years. Carl had been such a good husband—so patient, so supportive. The kennel had taken more time, more energy, more commitment, in short, more of his wife than either of them had bargained for.

No card, no present . . . nothing. She had given no

thought whatsoever to celebrating their anniversary—and tomorrow was to be their fifteenth. Knowing that she would be swamped with crisis control for the entire next day, she resigned herself to a sincere apology over coffee in the morning. Maybe she'd get lucky and discover that he had forgotten too.

Sleep sank in heavily and ended abruptly. In the darkness before the dawn, Kim rose with a soggy spirit. Not like the old days when she would spring out of bed anticipating the day's events. When she started the business, she had been thrilled at the challenges, inspired by each day's opportunities. But these days, her spirit seemed heavy, like her hips, and the weight, both physically and emotionally, had come on slowly and insidiously.

She shuffled into the kitchen to plug in the old, stained coffeemaker sitting on the counter. As the light over the sink came on, Kim's eyes adjusted to see a sparkling new coffeemaker with a bright red bow on top. A note attached read: "The greatest gift to my life is the gift of my wife. Love, Carl." Kim had been complaining about needing a new coffeemaker for weeks. The old one just wasn't keeping the coffee hot any longer.

Tears welled up in her eyes. After starting the brew, she

moved into the den to check the thermostat, and there stood a new lamp in the reading corner of the room with a big blue bow on it. The note read: "The greatest gift to my life is the gift of my wife. Love, Carl." Kim had wanted a floor lamp in her reading corner for a year now. It was on her Christmas list.

Now the tears spilled down her cheeks. She dropped into the big overstuffed chair under the lamp, overcome with emotion. As she reached for a tissue on the table beside the chair, she saw one more gift lying there. It was a very small box, wrapped most delicately and graced with a lavish gold bow on top. She opened it, sobbing. Brushing tears away with several sweeping strokes, she discovered an incredible sapphire necklace surrounded with tiny sparkling diamonds. The note read: "The greatest gift to my life is the gift of my wife. Love, Carl."

Kim ran to the room where Carl was sleeping. She fell onto the bed beside him and, still crying, apologized for her oversight and begged his forgiveness for her insensitivity. Carl lovingly drew her to him saying, "Kim, you have worked so hard and been such a tremendous example of diligence and perseverance for our children all these years. You have demonstrated an untiring devotion to us, to your staff, and to your animals. And you have made my life a wonderful place to live. You really are the greatest gift to my life. Trust me, I do not feel forgotten or neglected. I feel blessed above all men."

Kim will never forget their anniversary again. For that day has become in her memory a monument of love and devotion.

Affection

Never Forget

Near to Me

Inspiration

Vision

Enjoyment

Realization

Sweetheart

Adoration

Romance

Yesteryear

CHAPTER 3

Near to Me

Anniversaries are a time to stop and check the mile-markers by which to remember the journey. The road being traveled stretches like an endless highway when first starting out. Now, looking back, there is a ribbon of memories flowing behind. Those memories are a consistent reminder of the everyday wonders that comprise a marriage.

Sure, it's not always easy, but staying close creates an anchor to life.

Enjoy the journey.

ANNIVERSARY

THE POWER IS FOUND IN CONNECTION, THAT PROFOUND MEETING WHEN THE TRUEST PART OF ONE SOUL MEETS THE EMPTIEST RECESSES IN ANOTHER AND FINDS SOMETHING THERE, WHEN LIFE PASSES FROM ONE TO THE OTHER.

Larry Crabb

Affection

Never Forget

Near to Me

Inspiration

Vision

Enjoyment

Realization

Sweetheart

Adoration

Romance

Yesteryear

CHAPTER 4

Inspiration

It is a wondrous thing to find a best friend, a thing of beauty to love someone to the exclusion of all others. When friend and lover come together, the result is harmonious communication. God created each for the other, and for this we are eternally grateful.

Anniversaries are a perfect time to reflect on how little things bring friends and lovers together:

- a smile
- a wink
- holding hands
- a special laugh
- picking up the phone and hearing that familiar voice

Such a union inspires the best in all of us.

ANNIVERSARY

WHEN OUR RELATIONSHIPS
ARE BORN IN THE HEART OF
GOD, THEY BRING OUT THE
BEST IN US, FOR THEY ARE
NURTURED BY LOVE.

Don Lessin

IT ISN'T THAT I'M SUCH A
WONDERFUL HUSBAND AND FRIEND;
IT'S THAT SHE SEES ME THAT WAY.

Jim McGuiggan

◉ What a Difference
You've Made in My Life ◉

June 17 was coming on fast, and David wanted to make sure that this anniversary was a memorable one. David and Abby had been married for ten wonderful years—years that had passed by so quickly they seemed like the blink of an eye. He thought about going back to the little log cabin in the Smoky Mountains where they had spent their honeymoon, or perhaps he would splurge on a trip to Hawaii—he couldn't make up his mind.

One day as he was looking through a closet for some old clothes to wear while working in the yard, he saw it, his old dress blues from his days as a marine. The mere sight of the suit reminded David of the day he most remembered wearing it. He picked it up and pressed it to his face, inhaling deeply, trying to catch the fragrance of the garden he had taken Abby to so many years ago. It seemed he could still smell the honeysuckle and fresh flowers. It was June tenth, ten years ago. It was as unforgettable as the day he said "I do" just seven days later.

David closed his eyes and let the pictures of that evening run through his mind. Abby was the most beautiful girl in the town of Augusta, South Carolina. Her black hair, high cheekbones, and ever-present smile made her a standout no matter what setting she graced. However, it was Abby's high-spirited nature, sincere heart, and perpetual optimism that attracted the devotion of so many. She was being courted by no less than eight boys, several who were better looking than David, others who were wealthier, but none who loved Abby more than he. He wanted to marry her more than he wanted to breathe.

While at boot camp, he arranged for flowers to be sent to her every day of the week, and he made sure she received a letter from him every Saturday. Poetry filled each page, and every letter ended with, "Marry me and make me whole."

Abby would not consent to any of her suitors. She was looking for something she had not yet found in any of the young men who had requested her hand. Neither the flowers, the presents, the poetry, nor the promises moved her heart to say yes. When David came home from boot camp, his mission was sure. He had only a few weeks to persuade Abby to marry him, and he would pull out all stops to win her.

He asked her to give him a week of evenings to spend with just him. If after that time she did not want to marry him, he would accept her decision and go on to his new post. Every night found them at a different restaurant eating romantic dinners. They walked by the river, watched movies, and talked on her porch. And every night David would say to Abby, "Marry me and make me whole." To which Abby would simply shake her head no.

The last night they would be together was June tenth. David picked Abby up in his convertible, outfitted in his dress blues and ready for one more all-out assault to win the woman he loved more than life. She had said something to him about the man of her dreams that he totally understood. She had said, "I not only want a man who loves me; I want a man who realizes the inspiration I can be to his life, his dreams, and his work."

David drove Abby to a community garden that was in full bloom. Without saying a word, he spread a blanket for her to sit upon. He then looked into her deep brown eyes and said, "I have a message for you that comes straight from my heart. I am not much of a singer, but this song expresses how you have inspired me to be a better man."

With a voice that was soft and flat, but with a heart

overflowing with love, he sang the song "What a Difference You've Made in My Life." When he finished, he looked into eyes he had never seen cry and saw tears pooling and running down her cheeks. David tenuously said, "I ask you once more and never again, marry me and make me whole."

Abby stood and took his hands in hers, and with a voice full of emotion responded, "You are the one I have been looking for. The one whose life I can inspire with my love. You know what I will mean to your life, your dreams, and your work. Yes, yes, yes, I will marry you, and I will make you whole. And you will make me whole as well."

On this June seventeenth, Abby found herself amid the honeysuckle and flowers of that familiar garden. Driven there in a rented convertible by a man wearing dress blues. The same blanket was laid on the ground, and the same love was felt by a woman who heard a voice, soft and flat, once again sing "What a Difference You've Made in My Life."

Many *waters* cannot quench the *flame* of *love*, neither can the FLOODS drown it. If a *man* tried to *buy* it with *everything* he *owned*, he COULDN'T do it.

Song of Solomon 8:7 TLB

Affection

Never Forget

Near to Me

Inspiration

Vision

Enjoyment

Realization

Sweetheart

Adoration

Romance

Yesteryear

CHAPTER 5

Vision

It's been said that without a vision, people perish. The day two lives are joined together, there is a vision of the life to be led as husband and wife. Imagination gives way to the reality of what it's like to start each day side by side and to say good night to the moon arm in arm. The surprising thing is, reality outstrips the vision in so many ways.

All through life people long for this kind of relationship—a love that is farsighted enough to see that the best is yet to come, to believe that the vision of love can be the reality of life.

ANNIVERSARY

LOVE IS
A GREAT BEAUTIFIER.

Louisa May Alcott

A *wife* of
noble character,
who can *find*?
She is WORTH far more
than *rubies*.

Proverbs 31:10

Affection

Never Forget

Near to Me

Inspiration

Vision

Enjoyment

Realization

Sweetheart

Adoration

Romance

Yesteryear

CHAPTER 6

Enjoyment

In vibrant, joy-filled marriages there's seldom a dull moment. For those who choose to hold on for dear life, marriage is like a roller coaster—by far the most enjoyable ride in the park!

Be thankful for the pitfalls, for the unexpected twists and turns. Be thankful for the slow climbs and heart-stopping drops. Most of all, be thankful for having a partner for life. It's a pleasure to sit side by side as the "roller coaster cart" plunges through life.

Enjoy the adventure of every day.

ANNIVERSARY

TRUE INTIMACY MEANS
MAKING A SAFE PLACE TO SHARE
THE SECRET PARTS OF YOURSELVES—
YOUR HOPES, YOUR DREAMS, YOUR FEARS.

Joe Beam

Affection

Never Forget

Near to Me

Inspiration

Vision

Enjoyment

Realization

Sweetheart

Adoration

Romance

Yesteryear

CHAPTER 7

Realization

Sometimes the stresses and years cloud our minds and hearts, and we forget how much our mates mean to us. But then, a moment of realization awakens our dormant love, and we remember why we fell in love in the first place. It may come from a meaningful gaze over a newspaper or a secret smile over an "inside" joke. Or it may be found in a handful of wildflowers gathered on an impulse to say "I love you."

Realized love is a wonderful thing. It reminds us that God has supplied us with all we need to love the one we have chosen and to be loved in return.

ANNIVERSARY

THREE LITTLE WORDS, "I LOVE YOU,"
ARE THE WORDS THAT TOPPLE EMPIRES,
SHAPE DESTINIES, MAKE MEN
AND WOMEN RISK THEIR LIVES
AND UNITE MILLIONS OF COUPLES
IN HOLY MATRIMONY EVERY YEAR.
WHAT POWER IS IN THOSE WORDS!

Nancy Corbett Cole

WORK IS LOVE
MADE VISIBLE.

Kahlil Gibran

◉ Love Realized ◉

Why such a big deal over an anniversary? Chuck Miller was on his way home from a business trip, dreading the reunion with his wife, Melissa. He had forgotten their anniversary the day before, and Melissa had raised Cain over it on the phone the previous night. *A guy tries to make a good living for his family and gets his head chopped off for one little oversight*, he thought.

The problem was, Chuck hadn't overlooked their anniversary just this once. As a matter of fact, the last time he'd remembered it was their second anniversary. Yesterday had been their thirteenth. Melissa was weary of the insensitivity she read into his neglect. Did he love her or didn't he? To Melissa that seemed the obvious question.

To Chuck's way of thinking, there was no reason to ask the question and no real reason to set aside one day out of the whole year on which he must express how much he loved her. It made much more sense to him that he should just love her every day and let that be that. His love should be obvious. He was always doing things around the house: cleaning the garage, hosing down the deck, washing the cars—things that women didn't like doing.

The conversation the night before had really turned sour. It had left a bitter taste in Chuck's mouth. Melissa accused him of things that had never crossed his mind. He was hurt and angry. He wondered how someone with such a pampered life could be so demanding. And to think, he was the reason she had it so easy.

Melissa, on the other hand, was glad she had finally had the opportunity to air her feelings. She was tired of Chuck's irresponsible attitude toward their relationship. He seldom inquired about her feelings and rarely shared intimately with her. In fact, his definition of intimacy had been reduced to sex. What kind of jerk was he to think that she had no more depth, no greater need than mere physical fulfillment?

Those were the thoughts occupying the minds of the married couple residing at 2802 Rain Forest Drive. She was stewing over things at home, nurturing a grudge against him that was gaining momentum by the minute. He was fuming on an airplane, making his way from Los Angeles to the Chicago O'Hare airport, where his car had been parked for three days.

At 2:12 p.m., the television in Melissa Miller's den indicated an interruption in the usual programming for an announcement by the local news network. There had been a plane crash in a suburb outside of Chicago. Flight 1243 had originated in L.A. earlier in the day and was destined for a 2:35 arrival at O'Hare. Melissa caught the last few words of the news broadcast and began frantically changing channels to see if she could hear more details on another station. The phone rang. Her father, calling from his office in St. Louis, had heard the news while driving across town to a meeting. Wasn't Chuck due in from L.A. today? He had heard the entire report and filled Melissa in on the missing facts.

Melissa ran into Chuck's study. Surely there was an itinerary or a note scribbled somewhere with more flight information. Since she wasn't picking him up, there was no reason Melissa had needed to know the incidentals. It was a Thursday, so they didn't have plans for a social event. She just knew he would be home in time for the evening meal with her. Beyond that, nothing . . .

Chuck's plane had been slightly delayed due to weather in Chicago. There had been talk of postponing the flight until the next day. Storms had ravaged the Chicago area for several hours. Fall was setting in, and the cold-air/warm-air collision had brought on some nasty results. It reminded Chuck of he and Melissa's conflict. As far as he was concerned, she was the cold front—frigid was more like it. He considered himself warm and easygoing. If only Melissa would extend him the benefit of the doubt. He was a pretty likable guy by any standards. Every inch closer to home filled him with greater dread of facing the music over this forgotten anniversary. What's the big deal? He rehearsed the thought again in his mind . . .

Melissa called Chuck's secretary: "Phoebe, it's Melissa. Do you know anything about Chuck's flight from L.A. today? Did you make his arrangements?" Melissa groped.

Phoebe responded in her quiet, controlled voice, "No, Melissa. Chuck booked that flight over the Internet. I do know he's due in around 2:30 or so, if that's any help."

"No," came Melissa's dispirited reply. "I needed a flight number."

"Sorry, Melissa," Phoebe apologized. "Is something wrong?"

"I'm trying not to panic, Phoebe. But I just heard a news broadcast. A plane out of L.A. just crashed outside of the city. It was destined for O'Hare. I'm a little shaken, that's all," Melissa said, fighting back tears.

An obvious silence screamed through the phone. Phoebe was shaken too. Her loss for words said it all. "Melissa, let me see what I can find out around here. I'll call you back as soon as I can."

"Thanks, Phoebe. I'll be waiting."

Melissa hung up with an aching knot throbbing in her throat. *What am I going to do?* After trying Chuck's cell phone and getting no response, Melissa collapsed onto the couch and began to pray . . .

Chuck's plane taxied quite awhile before getting to an open gate. *I waste more time on airplanes these days,* he thought. At least he hadn't checked a bag. That was the only good thing that had happened to him in the past two days. He made a mad dash past all the reunions at the gate, wanting to avoid seeing the kind of affectionate embraces he knew he wouldn't be receiving when he got home. Out of the corner of his eye, he caught one passionate kiss exchanged between two lovers. Young and alive, the two of them reveled in their relationship. Chuck's heart stung with an empty anguish. The young woman reminded him of Melissa. He could remember days like that, when they were newly married. What had happened between them? Where had the love gone? . . .

Melissa's prayer turned into a long talk with the Lord about the man she had married. An athletic wonder in college, Chuck had kept his youthful figure and was just as handsome as the day they'd met, in spite of a trace of gray at his temples. The thing she loved most about him was the way he laughed. He laughed all the time! His laughter was so contagious and had blessed her life for all these years. Whenever she was sad, mad, or just down in the dumps, Chuck could make her laugh . . .

Chuck sped out of the parking garage. *Great!* he thought. *I forgot to recharge my cell phone, so I can't even call home to tell Melissa I'm on my way. It might be just as well. She's so mad at me, she'd just yell some more.* Chuck headed up the ramp on I-65 and began his battle with the pavement . . .

Melissa was sobbing and had gone to her knees. Chuck's plane should have landed by now, and he should have called on his cell phone. He always called when he got in. Considering their fight, she hoped he was just pouting, just holding out on her. *Oh Lord, please bring my Chuck home safely. I'm so sorry I was hard on him, Lord. He is such a good man. How could I overlook all the good in him over one little flaw. So what if he forgets our anniversary? He never forgets me, and isn't that the point, Lord? How could I have been so unkind, so unappreciative? . . .*

Chuck couldn't help but notice the wildflowers in the median. They were brilliant! He couldn't remember ever seeing them look like that. It was as if heaven had flung paint splotches all along the interstate in an incredible demonstration of color. Lavender, deep purple, and white, the flowers were waving cheerfully from the side of the road. They lifted his spirits just because they were there. Signs of life, hope, and joy. He contemplated how Melissa would love the look of them peppered all along the pavement . . .

Melissa's tears poured like rain. Her words had ceased. She had laid her heart bare before the Lord. He knew it all: how much she loved Chuck, how sorry she was for railing on him, how grateful she would be if the Lord would work a miracle of deliverance for her now. Her fear had paralyzed her. She could not move from her knees. There was nowhere else to turn . . .

Chuck explained to the state patrolman that he was obeying a romantic impulse. It was something he had to do. When he got to the part about forgetting his anniversary, the officer nodded his head and said, "I'm with ya, man.

I've been there myself. Just don't do it again, OK? You can't pull over on the side of the interstate to pull weeds." Chuck clutched the enormous bouquet of flowers to his chest and finished his drive home . . .

When Melissa heard the automatic garage door open, she gasped and jumped to her feet. Running through the kitchen, she burst through the door just as Chuck emerged with the bouquet of flowers. She ran to him and threw her arms around his neck, kissing his face and crying out loud: "I love you! I love you! Oh, Chuck, I'm so sorry I was mean to you. I just love you!"

Chuck was stunned. He thought to himself, *Man, if I'd only known all this time that all she needs is a handful of weeds off the side of the road!*

"Happy anniversary, honey," he said. "I love you too."

And *now* these
three remain:
faith, HOPE and love.
But the *greatest*
of these is love.

1 Corinthians 13:13

Affection

Never Forget

Near to Me

Inspiration

Vision

Enjoyment

Realization

Sweetheart

Adoration

Romance

Yesteryear

CHAPTER 8

Sweetheart

In an age when appearance is revered above what's in the heart, people who recognize the value of beautiful character and a lovely spirit enjoy the fruits of the "forever" kind of love. Vows solemnly made and reverently kept will bloom into a deep love that only true "sweethearts" know.

Anniversaries are a time to remember and be grateful for promises kept—promises to be sweethearts for life.

ANNIVERSARY

LOVE ISN'T JUST FOR
THE "BEAUTIFUL PEOPLE."
IT'S FOR ANYONE WITH A HEART.

Jim McGuiggan

AN ANNIVERSARY SAYS,
"THINK OF THE DREAMS YOU HAVE
WEATHERED TOGETHER. THEY ARE
INTIMATE ACCOMPLISHMENTS."

Charles R. Swindoll

◦ The Anniversary Tale ◦

John and Juanita had met by accident through the mail when John was serving in the military. Juanita was engaged to a friend of John's, and when John's friend decided to end the relationship, he asked John to write the letter for him. Juanita responded to John's letter a few days later, thanking him for the tenderness and compassion expressed in his words. She also asked if she could continue to write him. John consented immediately; and in the next few months, a romance ensued, motivated by the poetry, prose, and passion of the daily letters they wrote to each other.

The love blossomed and grew to the point that John admitted in a letter that he had fallen in love with Juanita. They had never exchanged pictures, and so he sent one of himself and asked if she would do the same. In her return letter, Juanita denied his request and told him that if his love were true, it wouldn't matter what she looked like. "However," she wrote, "you are very handsome."

With every letter, John fell more and more in love with

Juanita. In one of her letters, she wrote, "I sense that you are like a mountain stream that has been purified by the long hard journey from the peaks to the valleys. I am the pool at the end of the winding path, and you have brought refreshment and renewal to me. I love you very much."

John wrote back immediately and asked Juanita for her hand in marriage. Juanita said she would be honored to marry him. However, she was concerned that her appearance might not be to his liking. John answered as she thought he would—"I have fallen in love with your heart. Looks will not change who you are to me."

They agreed to meet at Union Station in New York City in two weeks. Since he did not know what she looked like, he asked her to carry a long-stemmed red rose. He would carry one as well; and when he saw her, he would give it to her and say, "May the joining of these two roses symbolize a fragrant and beautiful union that will last forever."

John arrived an hour early, wearing a brand-new trench coat and hat he had bought for the occasion. He was full of anticipation as the huge black train, spitting smoke and steam, rolled into the station. The platform quickly filled up with hundreds of people exiting the train and entering embraces of reunion with loved ones. John nervously paced up and down the platform, looking for the long-stemmed rose that would identify Juanita, the love he had waited for so long.

Suddenly he spotted a woman who appeared to be several years older than he who was carrying a long-stemmed red rose. He felt the sting of disappointment as she drew closer and her homeliness became more apparent. He repeated to himself what he had said in his letter: "I have fallen in love with your heart. Looks will not change who you are to me."

He quickly approached her and said, "May the joining of these two roses symbolize a fragrant and beautiful union that will last forever." The woman who was holding the rose gasped at the statement. "Young man, I don't know what this is all about, but the young lady who asked me to carry this rose said that if a man approached me with a similar rose, I should point her out to him. There she is over there."

As John turned, he beheld a beautiful black-haired woman with a beaming smile who was also holding a long-stemmed red rose. He walked slowly toward her, and with every step, her beauty became more and more evident. He extended the rose to the young woman, hoping with all of his heart to hear his name. He said, "May the joining of these two roses symbolize a fragrant and beautiful union that will last forever." To which Juanita answered, "It will, John, it truly will."

A *longing* fulfilled
is *sweet* to
the *soul*.

Proverbs 13:19

Affection

Never Forget

Near to Me

Inspiration

Vision

Enjoyment

Realization

Sweetheart

Adoration

Romance

Yesteryear

CHAPTER 9

Adoration

You've seen it on the faces of young people walking arm in arm, gazing into one another's eyes. Their young love is fresh and new, untainted by disappointments, unspoiled by broken dreams. But you've also seen it in the eyes of an old couple in the park, holding hands and laughing like children. They've traveled through disappointments and emerged victorious; they've survived broken dreams and built new and better ones. What is it that you see in their eyes? It's adoration.

Pure, unadulterated devotion. It's what lifelong love is made of.

Love is patient and kind.

Love is not jealous or boastful or proud or rude.

Love does not demand its own way.

Love is not irritable, and it keeps no

record of when it has been wronged.

It is never glad about injustice

but rejoices whenever the truth wins out.

Love never gives up,

never loses faith,

is always hopeful,

and endures through every circumstance. . . .

There are three things that will endure—

faith, hope, and love—

and the greatest of these is love.

1 Corinthians 13:4-13 NLT

ANNIVERSARY

YOU WILL FIND,
AS YOU LOOK BACK UPON YOUR LIFE,
THAT THE MOMENTS WHEN YOU HAVE
REALLY LIVED ARE THE MOMENTS
YOU HAVE DONE THINGS
IN THE SPIRIT OF LOVE.

Henry Drummond

Affection

Never Forget

Near to Me

Inspiration

Vision

Enjoyment

Realization

Sweetheart

Adoration

Romance

Yesteryear

CHAPTER 10

Romance

Old-fashioned love—the kind that makes room for only two—cherishes the little things. A meaningful gaze, a smile, a tender touch of the hand, simple exchanges fondly remembered. Such expressions of the heart convey security and enduring love, a love that provides a romantic sanctuary, a feeling of belonging.

Romance means that holding hands still melts hearts—long after the vigor of youth is gone—and longing gazes still fire the passions of love. Aren't you glad hopeful romantics still have a place in the world?

ANNIVERSARY

It is by loving and by being loved that one can come nearest to the soul of another.

George MacDonald

IN LOVE
THERE IS ALWAYS ONE WHO KISSES
AND ONE WHO OFFERS THE CHEEK.

French Proverb

☉ The Thirteenth Rose ☉

Mattie trudged up the aisle with the other passengers, eager to get off the plane. The flight was late, and a crowd waited inside the airport. Her eyes scanned the room for Sam. Disappointment flooded her heart when she realized he wasn't there to meet her. That wasn't like him.

Pushing through the throng toward baggage claim, Mattie finally spotted him standing at the edge of the crowd.

"I thought you'd never get here," he said simply, holding his arms open for a bear hug.

"That makes two of us," Mattie replied, grateful for the sight of his handsome face.

"Let's not go right over to the house," Sam said into her hair. "My parents can wait a little while longer. But something else can't."

Mattie gave him a teasing look.

"No questions," he said as he steered them out of the concourse to the parking lot.

Sam drove to the Italian restaurant where they had had their first date, just over one year ago. After opening Mattie's door and helping her out of the car, he reached into the backseat and pulled out a bouquet of beautiful red roses. Mattie's eyes lit up at the sight, but Sam playfully hid the roses behind his back. "Not yet, my love. Wait until we sit down." Taking Mattie's hand, he led her to the courtyard, where a table for two was prepared beside a fountain.

"Now, let me give you these properly," he said as he handed Mattie the roses.

Mattie smiled and buried her face in the roses, inhaling their sweet scent. Roses had always been her favorite. Instinctively, she counted the blossoms the way she counted everything.

"He made a mistake," she mused.

"What's that?" Sam said.

"The florist. He must have miscounted. There are thirteen roses, not twelve."

"One to grow on," Sam said mischievously, tapping one rose that was slightly larger than the others.

Then Mattie remembered—it had been exactly thirteen

months since they met on that blind date that almost didn't happen. A rose for every month.

Something sparkled in the bouquet. Mattie leaned closer, pushed the leaves aside, and saw a diamond ring, fastened by a red ribbon, on the stem of the thirteenth rose.

Affection

Never Forget

Near to Me

Inspiration

Vision

Enjoyment

Realization

Sweetheart

Adoration

Romance

Yesteryear

CHAPTER 11

Yesteryear

There is a kind of love that lasts beyond a lifetime—the kind of love that is built on shared hopes and dreams, mutually endured defeats and sadness. It's an everlasting love, based on commitment and caring and choosing to keep vows to cherish "for better or worse, in sickness and health, till death do us part."

And even when death does part two who've given their lives to each other, that love remains, filling the empty places with sweet memories of love and yesteryear.

ANNIVERSARY

No TIME OF LIFE IS SO BEAUTIFUL
AS THE EARLY DAYS OF LOVE
WHEN WITH EVERY MEETING,
EVERY GLANCE, ONE FETCHES
SOMETHING NEW HOME
TO REJOICE OVER.

Søren Kierkegaard

THE BEST AND THE MOST BEAUTIFUL THINGS IN THE WORLD CANNOT BE SEEN OR EVEN TOUCHED. THEY MUST BE FELT WITH THE HEART.

Helen Keller

◎ Attic Treasures ◎

Matilda Slocum stood at the attic doorway, leaning heavily on her cane as she peered up the steep stairs. Could she make it?

Well, she would try, and that was all there was to it. Today it mattered, more than any other day. For Henry's sake, she would try.

She took her first faltering step, then another. The ancient wooden stairs creaked as if outraged to have their slumber interrupted. It had been years since anybody had ventured up these stairs. After Henry got sick, he never went into the attic—why, he seldom left the bedroom they had shared for sixty-three years.

Matilda laughed inwardly. *These creaking stairs are just like my tired, old bones*, she thought. But she would try.

With a shuffling gait, she inched up the stairs, praying silently for safe passage to the top. When Matilda reached the attic floor at last, she stood for a moment, looking around her. Dust motes danced in a shaft of light from the single-dormer window. The wooden horse Henry had carved for the children stared from the far right corner, its eyes grown faint. This place was so full of memories.

Matilda blinked and wiped the back of her hand across her cheek.

She made her way across the room to the garment bag hanging from the rafters. Her wedding gown was inside—yellowed and moth-eaten but still exquisite with its hand-sewn beads. The veil had all but disintegrated, its tatters hanging like cobwebs from the headpiece.

But that wasn't what she was looking for. Where was that chest? A pile of dusty books obscured something in another corner. Going on a hunch, Matilda moved across the attic floor and dismantled the mountain of books one by one.

A sneezing fit momentarily stopped her progress. Then she saw it—the memory chest, as she had always called it. Matilda opened the heavy lid with its squeaking hinges gone black with time.

More memories flooded her mind as she worked her hands among the treasures: special projects from the children's school days, faded theater programs, a crushed corsage. Digging deeper, Matilda came to the manila pouch she had been looking for.

As she opened it, something slipped out. It was what she had come for—the treasure she had made this harrowing journey to the attic to retrieve: a handmade valentine, intricately cut in a lace pattern around the edges and illustrated with tiny cupids, flowers, and hearts. Henry had always been artistic. The day he gave her the valentine, on their first wedding anniversary, she caught a glimpse of just how deep his love for beauty ran. But it was Henry himself—the man—who had been so beautiful to her, and who still made her heart flip-flop, long after he was gone.

"To the one I love," he had inscribed in calligraphy.

"I love you too, Henry," Matilda whispered into the silent attic. "Happy Anniversary."

Express
YOURSELF!

Show how much you *care*

with these *heartfelt* books from the

BEST-SELLING HUGS™ LINE

Happy Anniversary!

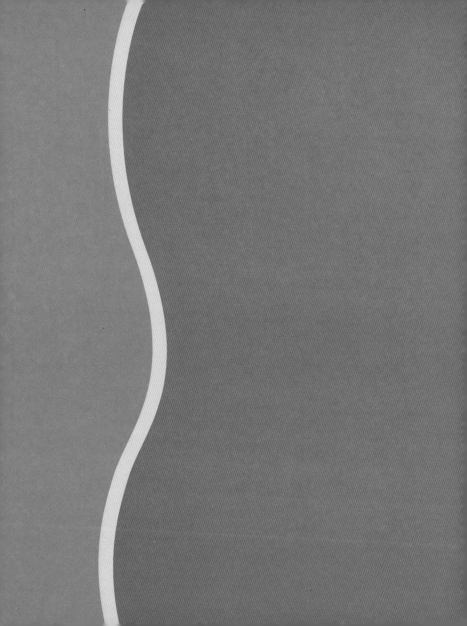